The Plymouth Colony

by Andrew Santella

Content Adviser: Professor Sherry L. Field,
Department of Social Science Education,
College of Education, The University of Georgia

Reading Adviser: Dr. Linda D. Labbo,
Department of Reading Education,
College of Education, The University of Georgia

COMPASS POINT BOOKS

Minneapolis, Minnesota

Photographs ©: North Wind Picture Archives, cover; Unicorn Stock Photos/Joe Sohm, 4; North Wind Picture Archives, 6, 7; Stock Montage, Inc., 8; North Wind Picture Archives, 11; Archive Photos, 12; North Wind Picture Archives, 15; FPG International, 17; Corbis/Burstein Collections, 19; North Wind Picture Archives, 20, 21; Archive Photos, 22, 23; North Wind Picture Archives, 25, 26, 27, 29, 30; Archive Photos, 32; North Wind Picture Archives, 33; Stock Montage, Inc., 35; North Wind Picture Archives, 36, 37, 38; Visuals Unlimited/Arthur Gurmankin, 39 top; North Wind Picture Archives, 39 inset, 40; Visuals Unlimited/E. Webber, 41.

Editors: E. Russell Primm and Emily J. Dolbear
Photo Researcher: Svetlana Zhurkina
Photo Selector: Dawn Friedman
Design: Bradfordesign, Inc.
Cartography: XNR Productions, Inc.

Library of Congress Cataloging-in-Publication Data

Santella, Andrew.
    The Plymouth Colony / by Andrew Santella.
        p. cm.— (We the people)
    Includes bibliographical references and index.
    Summary: Describes the reasons that the Pilgrims traveled to the New World, their voyage on the Mayflower, the hardships of their first winter in the Plymouth settlement, and the harvest celebration remembered as the first Thanksgiving.
    ISBN 0-7565-0046-X
    1. Massachusetts—History—New Plymouth, 1620–1691—Juvenile literature. 2. Pilgrims (New Plymouth Colony)—Juvenile literature. [1. Pilgrims (New Plymouth Colony) 2. Massachusetts—History—New Plymouth, 1620–1691.] I. Title. II. We the people (Compass Point Books).
    F68 .S25 2000
    974.4'8202—dc21   00-008675

TABLE OF CONTENTS

REACHING LAND

The Plymouth colony was the second permanent English settlement in America. The founding of the **colony** was something of an accident. The 102 settlers who started the Plymouth colony never planned to land near Cape Cod in Massachusetts. They had aimed for an area farther south.

A small reproduction of the Mayflower

4

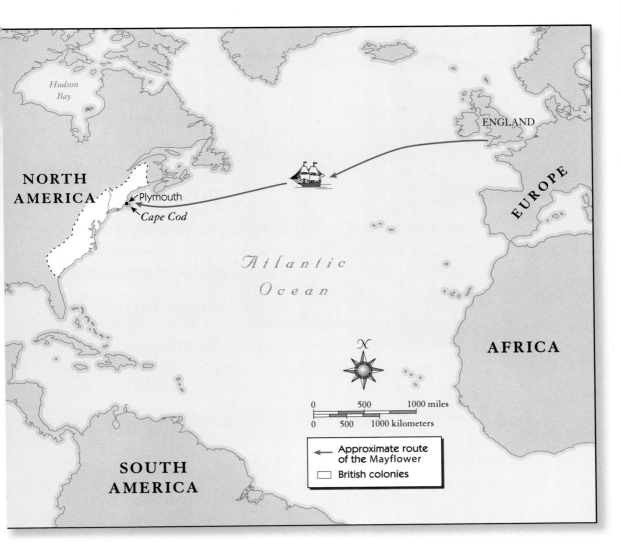

Hudson
Bay

ENGLAND

NORTH
AMERICA

EUROPE

Plymouth

Cape Cod

Atlantic
Ocean

AFRICA

N

0   500   1000 miles
0   500   1000 kilometers

← Approximate route
  of the Mayflower
☐ British colonies

SOUTH
AMERICA

Settling the Plymouth colony

Wilderness greeted the colonists at Plymouth.

But their ocean journey to North America had been cold, wet, and tiring. They had spent two months packed on a small ship called the *Mayflower*. And the hardships they had lived through in Europe made them ready for a new home—wherever it was.

So when they found a suitable spot for their settlement in November 1620, they decided to stay put in Massachusetts. Making a home there turned out to be even more difficult than what they had suffered through in Europe.

THE SCROOBY SEPARATISTS

Many of the founders of the Plymouth colony were members of the English Separatist Church. They believed that the only honest way to practice their religion was to separate from the Church of England.

King James I

There was one big problem, however. The Church of England was the country's official religion. The leader of the church and the leader of England were the same person—King James I. To break away from the Church of England was to break away from England itself. To many, that seemed like betraying the government, or treason.

7

The Separatists came from a small village in England.

Not surprisingly, the king and his government did not look kindly on **Separatists**.

One group of Separatists met in Scrooby, a little town in Nottinghamshire, England, in 1606. Later they came to be known as **Pilgrims**. A pilgrim is someone who makes a long journey,

8

sometimes as an act of religious faith. Indeed, these Pilgrims would one day travel all the way to North America. They were looking for a place where they could live and worship freely.

In England, government officials spied on the group's meetings. Many feared that they would be put in jail or even killed for their religious beliefs. The little community of believers began looking for a new home. They decided to move to Holland (now the Netherlands), where the government allowed more kinds of religious worship.

But without official permission to leave England, the Separatists would have to leave the country in secret. A group of them tried to leave in 1607, but they were discovered and jailed for a month. Finally, in 1609, they managed to leave England and settle in Holland.

LIFE IN HOLLAND

The Pilgrims did find freedom of religion in Holland. For twelve years, they lived there and met openly. They lived in Leiden, a city with a large university and a successful cloth industry. Every Sunday, they gathered for two sets of services—one from 8 A.M. to 12 P.M. and one from 2 P.M. to 5 P.M. The government did not interfere.

But life was not easy in Holland. The Pilgrims were, after all, living in a foreign country, with its own language and customs. As **immigrants,** many of them had to work at jobs that paid poorly and required hard labor.

Life was so difficult in Holland that the Separatists had a hard time convincing others to join them. Also, the threat of war between

10

The Separatists lived in a city in Holland called Leiden.

Holland and Spain was brewing. The Pilgrims

began considering another move.

    But where to go? England's colonies in

North America seemed promising. English

11

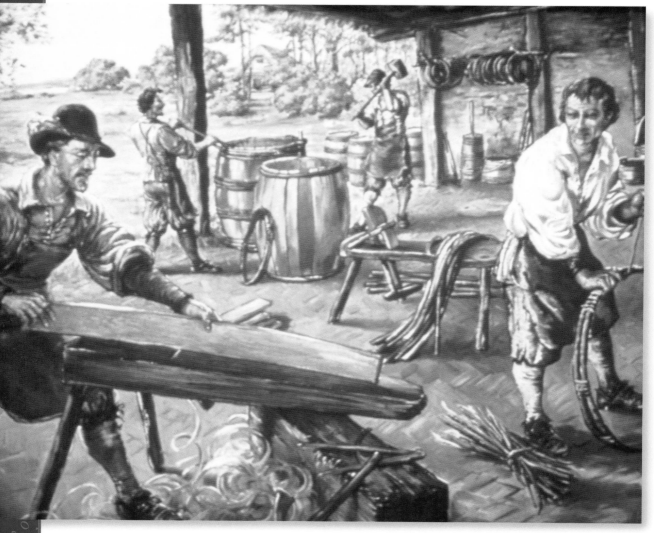

Colonists at work in Jamestown, Virginia

12

fishermen and traders had been traveling up and down the Atlantic Coast of North America for years. Some had even attempted permanent settlements.

Only one colony had survived though. English people had been living in Virginia since 1607. The colonists were not like the Pilgrims, however. Most of them were loyal to the Church of England. They had come to North America mainly to make money and find adventure.

Some of the Pilgrims in Holland feared the Virginia colonists as much as they feared the English government. They wanted to settle far from the Virginia colonists. They decided to head for what was then the very north of Virginia—the area around what is now New Jersey.

THEIR OWN SHIP

The Pilgrims still had to figure out how to pay for their journey to North America. They turned to a group of English **investors**. The investors agreed to put up the money and the Pilgrims promised to work hard at farming and fishing in their new home. After seven years, the investors and the Pilgrims would divide up the property and profits. The investors also signed up more English people who wanted to join the Pilgrims.

The Pilgrims bought a small ship, the *Speedwell*, to take them across the Atlantic Ocean. On July 21, 1620, they said goodbye to their friends in Holland. Before leaving, the **congregation** held a long prayer service. One of their leaders, William Bradford, later wrote, "So they

14

The Separatists left Holland by sea in 1620.

left that goodly and pleasant city which had been their resting place twelve years; but they knew they were pilgrims."

Before setting out for North America, the Pilgrims had to make one stop. They had to return to England to meet with the settlers signed

15

up by the investors. These settlers had hired their own ship, the *Mayflower*.

The final preparations for the trip were complicated. The Pilgrims and the investors had to work out the details of their agreement. The ships had to be loaded with everything from tools to weapons to trading goods. And the *Speedwell* had to be repaired. The little ship leaked badly. Every time the Pilgrims thought they had the problem fixed, another problem appeared. Twice they left for North America and had to turn back because of leaks. Finally, they left the troublesome *Speedwell* behind in the English city of Plymouth.

All 102 passengers squeezed onto the *Mayflower* for the journey across the Atlantic Ocean. The trip took sixty-seven long days. The *Mayflower* was often tossed about in storms and

Before the Pilgrims left, they prayed for a safe voyage.

rough water. Most of the passengers were seasick. All were wet and miserable. One storm cracked a beam on the *Mayflower* and caused some leaking. Some people talked of turning back and returning home. But they decided to press forward. Two of the travelers died on the ocean crossing, and one child was born—a boy named Oceanus Hopkins.

A New Home

On November 9, 1620, the *Mayflower* sighted land. It was Cape Cod in Massachusetts. Bradford wrote of the Pilgrims, "They were not a little joyful."

But the *Mayflower* was too far north. The *Mayflower's* captain tried to turn the ship, but the ship ran into rough waters. The captain decided to land.

Now the Pilgrims shifted their attention. For months, they had been thinking of surviving the ocean crossing. Now that they had made it safely to North America, they began thinking of how they would survive here. For one thing, they did not have permission from England to settle this far north. Until they could get the papers,

The Mayflower landing at Plymouth

The Mayflower Compact signatures

All the heads of household on the Mayflower signed the Mayflower Compact.

or **documents**, they needed from England, they would have to take matters into their own hands.

So, still on board the *Mayflower*, they wrote a document for every head of a household to sign. The signers pledged to be loyal to the king of England, but they also agreed to follow the wishes

21

of the community. Later, the document became known as the **Mayflower Compact**. It was the first written outline for government established in what is now the United States.

The signers of the document elected John Carver as their first governor. Then sixteen of the Pilgrims went ashore to look around.

Miles Standish led the group. He was one of the settlers invited to join the voyage by the English investors. His experience as a soldier in European wars made him a good choice for the group's military leader.

Miles Standish was a leader of the group.

Miles Standish and his scouting party

Standish and his men got their first glimpse of
Native Americans, but they were not able to make

contact with them. They also discovered a supply of corn and a kettle, which they took. They were not able to pay the owners back for another six months. Corn would turn out to be important to their survival.

Standish led several more trips along the coast, looking for a likely place to make a permanent home. The Native Americans on one occasion attacked Standish's men. The two groups shot arrows and muskets at one another, but no one was hurt. Finally, on December 11, 1620, a group went ashore at what is now Plymouth. They found fields already cleared and ready for farming and plenty of freshwater.

Word was sent back to the *Mayflower* that they had found a place to live. The ship and the

The Pilgrims prepare to land.

The Pilgrims finally arrive at Plymouth.

rest of the colonists arrived on December 16. According to legend, the Pilgrims landed at Plymouth Rock. But there is no record that this really happened.

Settlers work together to build a house.

The Pilgrims named the place *Plymouth*, after the city in England from which they had sailed. Then they set to work. They were far from home in an unknown place, and winter had set in. A few days before Christmas, they began building a fort and some simple houses.

That winter was deadly for the Plymouth colonists. They were worn out from their ocean journey. They had no fruits or vegetables to eat. Disease spread like wildfire. At one point, only seven Pilgrims were healthy enough to help the sick. In January 1621, the thatched roof of one building caught fire. No one was hurt, but some precious supplies were lost. When that winter finally ended, about half of the original group had died of illness, starvation, and cold.

Winter in Plymouth was difficult for the Pilgrims.

After their arrival, the settlers began to meet Native Americans.

MEETING THE NATIVE PEOPLE

In February 1621, the settlers began spotting Native Americans in the area, but for weeks none approached the settlement. Then on March 16, one man walked up to the tiny village. He was Samoset, a leader of the Abenaki people of Maine. In English, he said, "Welcome, Englishmen." Samoset had learned English from the cod fishermen who worked the Atlantic Coast.

He explained that he had traveled a long way and asked the Pilgrims for something to eat and drink. Then he began telling the Pilgrims about their new home. He explained why the fields were cleared but not used. After an outbreak of disease there a few years earlier, the local people had left.

Squanto was a Pawtucket Indian who helped the Pilgrims.

Samoset also told the Pilgrims which Indian tribes were peaceful and which were warlike.

About a week later, Samoset returned with another Native American, a Pawtucket named Squanto. Squanto spoke better English than Samoset. He had been captured by English explorers years earlier and sold into slavery in Spain. Somehow he escaped and made his way back to North America. Amazingly, he held no grudge against Europeans. In fact, Squanto acted as interpreter for the Pilgrims with other Native Americans.

Squanto helped arrange a meeting with Massasoit, the leader of the Wampanoag. The Pilgrims and Massasoit signed a peace treaty that

The Pilgrims and Wampanoag leader Massasoit sign a peace treaty.

lasted for more than fifty years. *Wampanoag* means "people of the dawn."

Squanto, Massasoit, and other Wampanoag showed the Pilgrims where to find fish and how to catch them. They also taught them how to plant and fertilize corn. The friendship the Pilgrims made with the Native Americans helped the Plymouth colony survive. And when Massasoit became very ill a few years later, it was the Pilgrims who nursed him back to health.

In April 1621, with the worst of the winter passed, the *Mayflower* returned to England. Only the hired crew was on board, however. All the surviving Pilgrims stayed on at Plymouth. The terrible winter had not defeated them.

The Native Americans showed the Pilgrims how to make the most of the land.

THE FIRST THANKSGIVING

That autumn, the Pilgrims harvested their first crops, including the corn that the Native Americans had taught them to plant. It was such a successful harvest that they planned a celebration. About ninety Wampanoag joined the Pilgrims for the

The Pilgrims and the Wampanoag celebrated their first harvest together.

36

The Plymouth colony in 1622

three-day-long event. They ate venison, roast
duck and goose, eels, clams, and even turkey.
The Pilgrims and the Wampanoag played games.
Years later, their celebration would become known
as the First Thanksgiving. To the Pilgrims, it was
simply a celebration of survival.

In fact, the Pilgrims had good reason to give
thanks. Just days after the celebration, another
ship appeared in the waters near Plymouth.

37

It was the *Fortune* and it brought more settlers to the colony. More colonists arrived on several more ships in the next few years. By 1627, the population of the colony was 150.

Their troubles were not over, of course. Lack of rain damaged their crops and sometimes there

The Pilgrims traded crops for furs with the Native Americans.

The Plymouth Colony Historical Museum tells the history of the colony.

The colony's first seal

was not enough to eat. The Pilgrims' agreement with their English investors ended in 1627. It left them owing money and in need of new ways to make their living.

More and more, the colony turned to farming and trade. Their good relations with the Native

39

A Pilgrim couple

Americans were important. They traded corn and other crops with the Wampanoag for beaver pelts. The Pilgrims, in turn, sold the beaver pelts to English traders for money to buy supplies. Other Pilgrims made their living fishing for cod or cutting timber for ships.

Over time, Plymouth did well. Two-story houses with shingled roofs and glass windows stood on each side of the main street. In 1652, the colony's leaders began building a new meeting-house. Meanwhile, other towns were springing up all around Plymouth. Each sent representatives to the colony's lawmaking group, the General Court. The General Court voted on laws and tried court cases. The governor of the colony and his **council**

Today, a memorial stands at the site of the landing at Plymouth.

presided over the General Court. Finally, in 1691, the Plymouth colony officially became part of the royal colony of Massachusetts.

The Pilgrims who came to Plymouth were not the first Europeans to settle in America, but they have come to represent the spirit of the colonists. They came from far away and risked their lives to live in freedom. Partly as a result of their hard work and determination, freedom and self-government became part of the American tradition.

GLOSSARY

colony—a group of people living in a new land with ties to a parent country; any of the thirteen British territories that became the original United States of America

congregation—people who meet for worship

council—a governing group

documents—official papers

immigrants—people who come to a foreign country to live

investors—people who provide money for a project in return for a share in the profits later

Mayflower Compact—an agreement signed by the men aboard the *Mayflower* establishing a local government

Pilgrims—the English settlers who came to Plymouth in 1620

Separatists—English people who preferred to separate from the Church of England

DID YOU KNOW?

- The Pilgrims first set foot on American soil at present-day Provincetown, Massachusetts, at the tip of Cape Cod.

- At the Thanksgiving feast of 1621, the Pilgrims did not use forks. They used knives, spoons, large napkins, and their fingers. They probably shared plates and drinking cups.

- Pilgrim children and adults probably took baths only a few times a year. They thought bathing was unhealthy.

- The term *Wampanoags* is never used. *Wampanoag*—or "people of the dawn"—is already plural.

IMPORTANT DATES

Timeline

1606	Pilgrims begin meeting in Scrooby, England.
1609	Pilgrims move to Leiden in Holland.
1620	Pilgrims cross the Atlantic Ocean on the *Mayflower* and establish Plymouth.
1621	Pilgrims and the Wampanoag celebrate harvest with what becomes known as the First Thanksgiving.
1627	Population of Plymouth grows to 150.
1691	The Plymouth colony becomes part of royal colony of Massachusetts.

Important People

William Bradford
(1590–1657), *Pilgrim leader*

John Carver
(1576–1621), *first governor of the Plymouth colony*

James I
(1566–1625), *king of England and leader of the Church of England*

Massasoit
(?–1661), *Wampanoag leader*

Samoset
(?–1653?), *Abenaki leader*

Squanto
(?–1622), *Pawtucket leader*

Miles Standish
(1584?–1656), *military leader of the Plymouth colony*

WANT TO KNOW MORE?

At the Library

Bowen, Gary. *Stranded at Plimoth Plantation, 1626.* New York: HarperCollins, 1994.

Collier, Christopher, and James Lincoln Collier. *Pilgrims and Puritans, 1620–1676.* New York: Benchmark Books, 1998.

Waters, Kate. *Samuel Eaton's Day: A Day in the Life of a Pilgrim Boy.* New York: Scholastic, 1993.

Waters, Kate. *Tapenum's Day: A Wampanoag Indian Boy in Pilgrim Times.* New York: Scholastic, 1996.

On the Web

For more information on *The Plymouth Colony,* use FactHound to track down Web sites related to this book.

1. Go to *www.facthound.com*

2. Type in a search word related to this book or this book ID: 075650046X.

3. Click on the *Fetch It* button.

Your trusty FactHound will fetch the best Web sites for you!

Through the Mail

Office of Travel and Tourism

100 Cambridge Street, 13th Floor

Boston, MA 02202

For information about travel in Massachusetts

On the Road

Plimoth Plantation

P.O. Box 1620

Plymouth, MA 02362

508/746-1622

To visit the seventeenth-century living history museum of Plymouth

INDEX

About the Author

Andrew Santella is a writer in Chicago, Illinois. He contributes to a wide
range of publications, including *Gentlemen's Quarterly*, the *New York Times
Magazine*, and *Commonweal*. He has written several books for children on
the history of America.